TO THE PEOPLE OF NEW YORK,

WHO WORK HARD EVERY DAY,

DO THEIR BEST TO RAISE GOOD CHILDREN,

ARE HONEST WITH OTHERS,

AND WANT TO LIVE IN A

PROSPEROUS STATE

Mark offers a blueprint for how we can restore New York's competitive standing. Failure to act will result in continued loss of our young people and consign the state to a dismal future of higher taxes and lower economic growth. The choice is ours.

—*John Faso, Candidate for New York State Governor*

This book allows the taxpayer to bypass the political spin and find out what really is wrong with the Empire State. Mark has pried open Pandora's Box with this book and New York is better for it.

—*Pat Manning, Assemblyman and founder of StandTallNewYork.org*

Mark has done New York State a valuable service by calling attention to the many challenges facing businesses in New York. These are the challenges government must meet for New York to achieve economic growth and prosperity.

—*Eliot Spitzer, NYS Attorney General*

Daily I confront the irresponsible legislation emanating from Albany. Mark is dead on. Our state leaders ignore the majority's interests, serve the special interests, and unwittingly diminish our future. Many of Mark's ideas would dramatically improve our government's effectiveness, children's education, businesses' competitiveness, and citizens' well being.

—*Tom Suozzi, Nassau County Executive*

Mark has deftly articulated New York's "Gordian Knot." His book demonstrates a thorough understanding of the problems New York businesses face, which New York's government must address – now!

—*Honorable William F. Weld*

This is an important book which illustrates exactly how the state's dysfunctional government hurts the business climate and the quality of life in our state. Mark is a critical ally in our fight to fix New York State government and restore fiscal sanity to Albany.

—*David A. Paterson, NYS Minority Senate Leader*

Here are good ideas to get New York back on track from an unusual source: someone who actually has to meet a payroll and is trying to grow a business. Mark's ideas deserve the careful attention of state leaders.

—*Jay Gallagher, Capitol Bureau Chief, Gannett News Service, Author of* The Politics of Decline: How Citizens Can Save New York

It's easy to complain about New York State Government, but it's hard to change it. Mark has thoughtfully created a solid reform package to create positive change. He's earned our respect. He needs our help.

—*Jim Walsh, U. S. Congress*

Mark writes a thoughtful analysis of the problems facing our state and a framework to solve these problems. This is a remarkable book that is a must read by all New Yorkers who are concerned for the future of our state.

—*Charles Nesbitt, Former NYS Minority Assembly Leader*

Opinion polls frequently remind us a majority of New York residents feel the Empire State is on the wrong track. Mark has done an absolutely superb job of documenting *why* this feeling is justified — and to pointing to the reforms needed to put the state on the right track.

—*E.J. McMahon, Empire Center for NYS Policy*

Everyone in New York should read Mark's book and RUN, not walk, to their nearest polling place. Your legislator is probably one of the nicest people in the world, but if they're not part of the solution that Mark prescribes, then they are part of the problem and need to be removed.

—*Bruce Grieshaber, Jenna's Law*

Mark concisely describes and offers solutions to the state government's shortcomings. His solutions lift burdens from businesses, encourage them to remain in the state, and enable all of us to prosper.

—*Michael Long, Chairman of the NYS Conservative Party*

This is a guidebook to constructive change. It is straightforward, insightful, and filled with common sense. Mark leads us away from political maneuvering and toward real leadership.

—*David Little, NYS School Board Assoc. Director of Governmental Relations*

Anyone who cares about NYS should read this book. It should be read by every candidate for governor, every legislator, every legislative staffer, and every newspaper editorial board. Mark describes the problems, identifies sensible solutions, and issues a challenge. Do we have the courage to change a system that suits the powerful and thrives on the status quo?

—*Mark Alesse, State Director, National Federation of Independent Businesses*

This book should be on the desk of every New York State business owner and legislator.

— *Jack Endryck, Managing Director, Building Industry Employers of NYS*

This book provides thoughtful assessment of the challenges facing our state. It is time to move from word to deed and for all of us — public, private and legislative, to collaborate, solve these challenges, and ensure a prosperous future for our state.

— *Linda Sanford, Chairwoman, The Business Council of New York State*

Mark has the uncanny ability to simply state, complex problems, and offer practical solutions that will return New York to its Empire State status for future generations!!

— *David Duerr, Interim President, Greater Syracuse Chamber of Commerce*

This book is about our lost ability to compete on an equal footing with five billion other people who have the U.S. in their economic sights. It is ironic the Empire State has fallen from the top to the bottom of our country. Burrows Paper is only 30% left in NYS. We must reverse the insidious degradation of our state.

— *Bill Burrows, Owner and President of Burrows Paper*

Mark is a welcome addition to the reform movement in New York State. His knowledge of small business and passion for needed reform make him a force to be reckoned within this movement.

— *Barbara Bartoletti, Legislative Director, League of Women Voters of NYS*

Mark has been a national and state leader in the agriculture for years. His past successes and thought provoking book are evidence that he can help us build a better New York State. His thoughts need to be discussed and debated, but frankly the state's implementation of most of them is long overdue.

— *John Lincoln, President of New York State Farm Bureau*

This is impressive plain spoken advice from a sixth generation farmer with a solid grounding in economics and pubic policy. His objective is clear – rebuild a better state for future generations. It's time to get behind his ideas, revitalize the state's economy, and improve the well-being of all New Yorkers.

— *David Klein, CEO, The Lifetime Healthcare Companies*

Table of Contents

Preface

Part I: The Gordian Knot
Do Any of Our Leaders Look at the Data? 1
Vested Interests 3
Higher Business Costs 4
Loss of Businesses, Capital, Talent, and Youth 5
Rigging the System and Evading Accountability 5
Economic Decline 8
Imagining a Different Future 10

Part II: Voter Bill of Rights
Voter Initiative 11
Non-partisan Voting Districts 12
Citizen Based Campaign Financing 12
Senate & Assembly Rule Reforms 15

Part III: Taxpayer Bill of Rights
Interstate Benchmarks & Performance Based Compensation 17
Public Sector Borrowing and Spending Limits 20
Reining in Medicaid 21
Consolidation of Local Government 23

Part IV: Inner City & Rural Student Bill of Rights
Equitably Fund All Public Schools 25
Strengthen School Administrations 27

Part V: Business Bill of Rights
Competitive Electrical and Workers Compensation Costs 32
A Competitive Tort Environment 34

Part VI: Igniting an Economic Renaissance 37

Initiative Summary 41
Table References & Notes 46
Endnotes 49
Acknowledgements 54
About the Author 56

The fault, dear Brutus, is not in our stars,
but in ourselves, that we are underlings.

— William Shakespeare

Preface

People often remark that "nothing will change in Albany" or that "there is nothing we can do about Albany." This pessimism and resignation always makes me cringe inside and recall my 1979 experience in Eastern Europe, and my 1981 experience in Poland.

In 1979, on a university sponsored travel study program through Europe, I found pessimism and resignation among the Eastern Europeans toward life in their countries, their communist rulers, and the U.S.S.R. At the time, no one imagined the Poles would soon confront their communist leaders and a world superpower. No one foresaw that the Soviet Union would unravel, and East and West Germany would reunite. All one heard is "life is miserable under communism and nothing is going to change."

Yet in 1981, heartened by the elections of Pope John Paul II and President Reagan, the Poles stood up to their leaders' tyranny, poor performance, corruption, and endless conflicts of interest. Right before my eyes, I witnessed what people can accomplish when they courageously stand together.

The thoughts within this booklet are merely a pebble in the vast sea of rhetoric. Yet, their implementation would end New York State's slow economic death spiral and ignite a tremendous economic renaissance. The thoughts may slowly dissipate. Or with your help, they may steadily garner support. They may even grow into an enormous wave of change with unimaginable consequences.

My years in Poland taught me to believe in the unforeseen. They taught me that tyranny and corruption are transitory, and that individual acts do matter. So let us press forward and encourage our friends to press forward. A democratic and prosperous New York State is a worthy end, and its pursuit is more exhilarating than resignation and complacency.

Part I: The Gordian Knot

A world of vested interests is not a world which welcomes the disruptive force of candor.

Agnes Repplier

Do Any of Our Leaders Look at the Data?

In just 50 years, the number one economy in the world has been reduced to 44th among the 50 states. New York State now ranks 45th in Personal Income Growth, Population Growth, and Employment. We rank 32nd in People without Health Insurance and 41st in Poverty. We spend the most per pupil educating our children, but rank 44th in the percent of students graduating from high school, and 43rd in student SAT Scores. We have the longest commute times to work and the 45th highest percentage of bridges in need of repair. Clearly, New York standards of living are declining relative to other U.S. residents (Table 1).

Many attribute New York's poor performance to its climate and the economic rise of the South, Mexico, and China. Yet, Minnesota, farther north and with a harsher climate, ranks high among the fifty states in almost every category. Minnesota is 1st in the percent of its population employed and covered with health insurance. It has the 2nd lowest Poverty Rate and 2nd fewest Deficit Bridges. Minnesota ranks 3rd in Personal Income Growth and 19th in Population Growth. It has the 15th lowest Per Pupil Education Cost, but the 3rd highest Graduation Rate and 6th highest SAT scores. It has the 18th shortest Commute Time.

Table 1: Pataki's, Bruno's, and Silver's New York State

50 State Rank	NYS	Minnesota
Personal Income[a] Annual Growth 1994-2003	45th	3rd
Population[a] Annual Growth 1994-2003	45th	19th
Employment[b]	45th	1st
Health Insurance[b]	32nd	1st
Poverty Rate[b]	41st	2nd
Education Cost[b]	50th	15th
Graduation Rate[b]	44th	3rd
SAT Score[b] Ave Math & Verbal 2004	43rd	6th
Commute Time[b]	50th	18th
Deficit Bridges[b]	45th	2nd
Composite Ranking	44th	8th

[a] Department of Commerce Bureau of Economic Analysis;
[b] A Statistical View of the United States: State Rankings 2005

New York's fifty year decline has been caused by what might be thought of as an entanglement of a few powerful interests. This entanglement, or Gordian Knot, causes the state to underperform other states. The knot causes our representatives' interests to be unaligned with the people's interests. It prevents the New York legislature from resolving systemic income, employment, healthcare, poverty, education, and transportation challenges.

Vested Interests

The knot's entanglement stems largely from an insidious exchange. *The Governor, Senate Majority, and Assembly Majority exchange preferential laws, mandates, and benefits for large campaign contributions with vested interests.* The importance of the exchange is evidenced by the 3.5 times increase in lobbying expenditures during the last 10 years. In the 2003-04 election cycle alone, lobbyists spent $264 million to influence elected officials in New York State (Table 2).

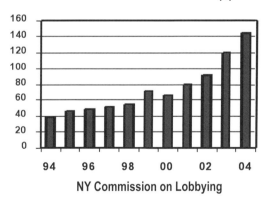

Table 2: Millions Spent Lobbying NY State & Local Government ($)

NY Commission on Lobbying

Higher Business Costs

These actions cause businesses to incur higher costs, lower returns, and lower valuations than businesses in most other states. The New York Business Council estimates the cost of settling a workers' compensation case in New York State runs 72% over the national average. Electricity and natural gas are 57% and 37% higher than the national average. Property taxes are 45% and liability insurance 28% above the national average (Table 3).

Table 3: NYS Business Costs
Amount Above the National Average

Workers' Comp Case 2004[a]	72%
Electricity Cost 2004[a]	57%
Natural Gas Cost 2004[a]	37%
Property Tax 2002[b]	45%
Liability Cost[a]	28%

[a] The Business Council of New York State;
[b] A Statistical View of the United States: State Rankings 2005, Morgan Quitno.

These higher business costs are tragic, because elected officials inflict them on their constituents. They are tragic because they cause well-established, excellent businesses to leave the state. They are tragic because they cause fewer people to be employed, expand the social service roles, and force large numbers of our families and friends to leave the state.

The governor and majority party incumbents respond to New York's business woes by creating corporate welfare programs rather than addressing the state-induced high costs of doing business. These misguided efforts rescue a few high profile and politically supportive businesses, but do not help thousands of other businesses across the state. Many of the ignored businesses respond to New York's higher costs by outsourcing, expanding in other states, and relocating.

Loss of Businesses, Capital, Talent, and Youth

The higher business costs cause entrepreneurs, youth, jobs, and capital to flee to other states, while New York's dependent population increases. The Federal Reserve of New York State estimates that from 1983 to 2002, the U.S. added 37% more high skilled manufacturing jobs, while New York State lost 14% of these jobs. From 1993 to 2003, the state's population grew 5%. The population between the ages of 25 and 44 decreased 3%, and the population 65 and older grew 22%. During the same time period, New York's Medicaid population increased a whopping 33% (Table 4).

Rigging the System and Evading Accountability

Meanwhile, the New York Senate and Assembly Majorities institutionalize their advantages and evade accountability. The Republican Senate majority draws its voting districts so it routinely wins 34 of the 62 seats by a 25% margin. Similarly, the Democratic Assembly majority draws its voting districts so it routinely wins 87 of the 150 seats by a 25% margin. To elect a minority party candidate in the majority controlled districts, twenty-five percent of the population must cross party lines (Table 5).

Table 4: The Productive & Young Flee while the Dependent Population Grows

	U.S.	NYS
High Skilled Manufacturing Job Growth 1983-2002[a]	37%	-14%

The Pataki, Bruno, & Silver Years: 1993-2003	
Total Population[b]	5%
Ages 25-44[c]	-3%
Ages 65 & Over[c]	22%
Growth of Medicaid Enrollment [c]	33%

[a]Buffalo Branch, Federal Reserve of New York State, Regional Economy, Winter 2004; [b]U.S. Department of Commerce, Bureau of Economic Analysis; [c]State Rankings 1995 & 2005, Morgan Quitno; US Bureau of the Census.

Table 5: Gerrymandering Ensures Majority Party Senate & Assembly Control

	Districts with > 25% Victory Margin in 2002	District Wins Needed for a Majority
Republican Senate	34	32
Democratic Assembly	87	76

"Reform New York: Redistricting,"
New York Public Interest Research Group

Economic Decline

From 1950-2003, New York State's share of U.S. income declined 37%. Over the same period, the northern states of Minnesota and New Hampshire maintained or increased their shares of U.S. income (Table 6).

Table 6: New York's 50 Year Decline

Share of U.S. Income	[a]1950	[b]2003	Change
New York	12.0%	7.6%	-37%
Minnesota	1.9%	1.9%	0%
New Hampshire	0.3%	0.5%	67%

[a]U.S. Department of Commerce, Bureau of Economic Analysis; [b]U.S. Bureau of the Census

New York's income growth has continued to lag other states under Governor Pataki, Majority Leader Bruno, and Speaker Silver. From 1994-2003, Upstate New York's per-capita income adjusted for inflation increased a paltry $2,800 and Downstate New York increased $4,700. During the same time period incomes in Minnesota increased $5,500. *If New York incomes had grown as much as Minnesota incomes, a New York family would earn on average an additional $4,600 each year.* Collectively, New York residents would earn an additional $26 billion each year (Table 7).

Table 7: Income Growth
The Pataki, Bruno, & Silver Years: 1994-2003

	[a]Inflation Adjusted Per-Capita Income Change
[b]Downstate NY	$4,700
Upstate NY	$2,800
Minnesota	$5,500

[a]U.S. Department of Commerce, Bureau of Economic Analysis; U.S. Department of Labor, Bureau of Labor Statistics; [b]Downstate is defined as Putnam, Westchester, Rockland, Nassau, Suffolk, Bronx, New York, Richmond, Kings, and Queens counties.

Vested interests use campaign contributions to buy laws, mandates, and benefits from the Governor, Democratic Assembly, and Republican Senate. The laws, mandates, and benefits raise Workers' Compensation, Energy, Property, and Liability costs to such an extent that many New York businesses are unable to compete with businesses outside of the state. Business leaders respond by moving capital, facilities, and jobs to other states and countries. The Democratic Assembly and Republican Senate rig the system to evade accountability and solidify the entanglement. This is New York State's Gordian Knot. People sense the knot, but do not fully understand its degenerate effects, or what to do about it.

Imagining a Different Future

Let us imagine for a minute a prosperous future. This future provides better paying jobs and enables all New Yorkers to more easily make ends meet. This future improves the likelihood that our children and grandchildren find opportunity in New York State, and that we will not have to spend hundreds of dollars and numerous days traveling to visit them.

In this prosperous future a robust job market covers another one million New York residents with health insurance. Adequately funded inner-city and rural education better prepare more youth for 21st century jobs. The strong state economy draws another 10% of our young people graduating from high school into the job market and off the social service roles.

In this improved future, we commute to work on roads and bridges in good repair. We reduce our commute times to work by 5 minutes each way. This seemingly small change frees up 42 hours a year for each of us, collectively reduces our commuting time by 375 million hours a year, and decreases our fuel consumption by some 400 million gallons a year.

This future is obtainable with a New York government that aligns representatives' interests with the people's interests and with honest, focused, competent leadership. As the data in Table 9 on page 16 demonstrates, Minnesota currently enjoys this prosperous future. The policies of Minnesota further prosperity for its population far better than those of our state.

Part II: Voter Bill of Rights

Every government degenerates when trusted to the rulers of the people alone. The people themselves therefore are its only safe depositories.

— Thomas Jefferson

The preceding data suggests that four groups, Voters, Taxpayers, Students, and Businesses fair poorly in New York State. For New York State to prosper, elected officials must address the challenges these groups face. The Voter Bill of Rights, comprised of Voter Initiative, Non-partisan Voting Districts, Citizen Based Campaign Financing, and Assembly & Senate Rule Reforms, addresses the disenfranchisement of voters.

Voter Initiative

Elected representatives do not implement policies that limit their tenure and compensation, nor their ability to borrow, tax, and spend. They do not pass policies that make elections competitive. Being mostly attorneys, representatives do not enact policies that constrain litigation.

Voters need a mechanism to further their interests when they collide with the elected officials' self interests. Voter Initiative provides this mechanism by enabling citizens, who obtain enough supporting signatures, to propose laws to voters in the general elections.

The process should be sufficiently difficult to avoid frivolous initiatives, but not so difficult to discourage needed initiatives. Requiring 32,000 supporting signatures, or 500 from each of New York's 62 counties, would permit a few widely supported initiatives to come before the voters each year (I-1).

Non-partisan Voting Districts

Majority incumbents have transformed the legislature from the people's agent to their agent. The Senate and Assembly district lines reveal intent to manipulate the democratic process and contempt for the will of the people.

Majority parties draw district lines to benefit their members. The Senate, controlled by the Republicans, packs as many Democrats into as few districts as possible. Similarly, the Assembly, controlled by the Democrats, packs as many Republicans into as few districts as possible. This practice enables majority parties to win a majority of the districts by comfortable margins.

The New York Public Interest Research Group indicates that party leadership in New York State has not changed in either house in over 30 years. In 2002, 182 of 212 districts were won by greater than a 25% margin. Incumbents have lost only 35 of 2544 races in the last 24 years. Incumbents had no major party opposition in over one-third of the races in the last election.[1]

To correct this cooption of our representative democracy, an independent commission of retired judges could oversee the development of a computer algorithm to draw Senate and Assembly districts. The algorithm would maximize the use of county, city, borough, township, and village lines and minimize the number of lines to draw each district (I-2).

Citizen Based Campaign Financing

The Governor, Republican Senate Majority, Democratic Assembly Majority, and the special interests exchange preferential laws, mandates, and benefits for large campaign contributions. *In the last 10 years, lobbying expenditures increased by 350%.* The largest spenders are the NYSUT (teachers union), 1199-SEIU (health care workers union),

LAWPAC, Medical Society, Empire Dental, NYSCOPBA (police and prison guard union), HANYSPAC (health care providers), AFL-CIO, Public Employees Union, NYC Carpenter's Union, RSA (New York City landlords), and Civil Service Employees' Union (Table 8).

Table 8: NYS PACS Largest Contributors 2004

NYSUT (Teachers Union)	$1,321,000
1199/SEIU (Health Care Workers Union)	$775,000
LAWPAC (Attorneys)	$771,000
Medical Society (Doctors)	$519,000
Empire Dental (Dentists)	$410,000
NYSCOPBA (Police & Prison Guards Union)	$353,000
HANYS PAC (Healthcare Providers)	$312,000
AFL-CIO Union	$247,000
Public Employees Union	$246,000
NYC Carpenter's Union	$235,000
RSA (NYC Landlords)	$202,000
Civil Service Employees' Union	$184,000

Political Action Committees Contributions in New York State 2004,
New York Public Interest Research Group

Six of the twelve largest campaign contributors are public sector unions. Terry Moe, professor and department chair of the Political Science Department at Stanford writes:

Public sector unions . . . are extraordinarily powerful. They have many millions of members, they are loaded with money for campaigns and lobbying, and they have activists in virtually every political district in the country. No other interest group can match their potent combination of money, manpower, and geographical dispersion . . .

On the surface, these unions may come across as a benign presence in our midst. After all, they represent teachers, nurses, and other government employees who perform services that are valuable, sometimes indispensable, to all of us. What's good for them would seem to be good for us – right? The problem, however, is that this is not even close to being right. What's good for them is sometimes quite bad for us.

At the heart of this problem is a genuine dilemma of democratic government: As governments hire employees to perform public services, the employees inevitably have their own distinctive interests. They have interests in job security and material benefits, in higher levels of public spending and taxing, and in work rules that restrict the prerogatives of management. They also have interests in preventing governmental reforms that might threaten their jobs. To the extent public employees have political power, therefore, they will use it to promote their own job-related interests - which are not the same as, and may easily conflict with, what is good for the public as a whole.[2]

To mitigate the tacit exchange of preferential laws, mandates, and benefits for large campaign contributions, we need to insist our representatives enact Citizen Based Campaign Financing. Citizen Based Campaign Financing allows candidates to raise campaign funds only during the ten months prior to an election; requires them to return any unused campaign funds to donors after an election; bars businesses, unions, PACs, and all organizations from making campaign contributions; and limits individual contributions to $100 per candidate per year (I-3).

Senate & Assembly Rule Reforms

Majority Leader Bruno and Speaker Silver have transformed the governing process in each house from a democratic one to an autocratic one, from one that serves the people to one that serves the majority parties' self interests.

The Majority Leader and Speaker control each of their party members by controlling committee assignments, member staffs and budgets, lulus, and member items. They reward and punish members by controlling the money representatives bring home to their districts. These member items are the primary means for representatives to obtain public recognition and favor with their electorate.

In New York, members draft hundreds of bills that have no chance of passing in order to appear to care about issues important to their constituents. A few well-organized groups make significant contributions to the Republican Senate or Democratic Assembly parties. The Majority Leader and Speaker release the few bills favored by these special interests. Input from the public is not obtained. There is little debate and no amendment of bills. The Majority in both houses approve in a rubber stamped manner the bills the Majority Leader and the Speaker release.

The Brennan Center for Justice indicates that from 1997 to 2001 the Senate and Assembly held only six public hearings for every 1000 bills, and committees submitted eleven research reports for every 1000 bills. More startling, the Senate passed all of the 7,109 bills that came to the floor, and the Assembly passed all of the 4,365 bills that came before it. Not a single bill was defeated on the floor. Not a single bill of the 308 major bills that became law was amended in either house.[3]

The Senate and Assembly Rule Reforms recommended by Jeremy Creelan in "The New York State Legislative Process:

An Evaluation and Blueprint," reduce special interest influence, expand representative participation, and elevate the quality of the legislative process.

More specifically, a) Senate and Assembly Rule Reforms end voting district and remuneration inequities by treating all senators and assembly members equally within their respective houses with regard to their budget, staff, member item money, and compensation. b) Require any exceptions made for house and committee leaders to be approved by two thirds of the members in both the Senate and Assembly. c) Empower committee chairs to employ and terminate staff; require committees to hold a public hearing upon the request of one quarter of the committee members; and require committee chairs to hold votes to release each bill referred to the committee 60 days prior to the end of a session. d) Make the votes part of the public record. e) Require a complete committee report for all bills favorably reported by a committee; require a house floor vote on every bill that is favorably discharged from a committee within 60 days; and convene conference committees upon the request of either of a bill's major sponsors (I-4).[4]

These four initiatives, Voter Initiative, Non-partisan Voting Districts, Citizen Based Campaign Financing, and Assembly and Senate Rule Reform, comprise my Voter Bill of Rights. The initiatives give voters more say and special interests less. They weaken the hold majority party representatives have on incumbency and the legislative process. They distribute power from the legislative leadership and organized special interests to the voters and their representatives.

Part III: Taxpayer Bill of Rights

The art of taxation consists in so plucking the goose as to obtain the largest possible amount of feathers with the smallest possible amount of hissing.

— Jean Baptiste Colbert

Implementing the Voter Bill of Rights initiatives discussed in the previous section lays the groundwork for enactment of the Taxpayer Bill of Rights discussed in this section. The Taxpayer Bill of Rights includes: Interstate Benchmarks and Performance Based Compensation, Public Sector Borrowing and Spending Limits, Reining in Medicaid, and Consolidation of Local Government. The Taxpayer Bill of Rights initiatives would transform economic decline into robust economic growth. They would create and free resources to improve the state's inner-city and rural schools, as well as transportation infrastructure.

Interstate Benchmarks & Performance Based Compensation

We generally do not take the time to evaluate how our state is doing relative to other states or assess the effectiveness of our leaders. *As businesses benchmark against their competitors, we must benchmark the effectiveness of our state and its leaders against other states and their leaders.*

Table 9 compares New York's and Minnesota's Personal Income and Population Growth, Employment, Healthcare, Poverty, Education, and Transportation. The comparison indicates Minnesota's personal income and population grew substantially more the last ten years. Most striking though, is the fact that Minnesota employs 72% of its population, while New

York only employs 58%! Rates of unemployment do not tell the story. New York's unemployment rate is similar to other states, but its employment rate is well below the national average.

Also striking are the facts that New York's uninsured population and poverty rate are twice those of Minnesota's. An extremely sad and related fact is although New York State spends far more per pupil on elementary and secondary education than any other state, average graduation rates and SAT scores are lower than the national average.[5]

Table 9: Our State Leaders Can Do Better

	NYS	Minnesota
Personal Income[a] Annual Growth 1994-2003	3.8%	4.5%
Population[a] Annual Growth 1994-2003	0.4%	1.1%
Employment[b] % of Population 2004	58%	72%
Health Insurance[b] % Uninsured 2003	16%	8%
Poverty Rate[b] % of Population 2003	14%	7%
Education Cost[b] Per Pupil 2004	$12,270	$8,920
Graduation Rate[b] High School 2004	59%	85%
SAT Score[b] Ave Math & Verbal 2004	1007	1180
Commute Time[b] Average 2003	30 min	22 min

[a]U.S. Department of Commerce, Bureau of Economic Analysis;
[b]A Statistical View of the United States: State Rankings 2005, Morgan Quitno.

Representatives spend far too much time hosting fund raisers, currying favor with large campaign contributors, and squabbling among themselves. They spend far too little time analyzing the data, learning the best practices of other states, holding public hearings, and working together creatively to further their population's well-being. New York leaders need to watch these benchmarks and enact policies that will further prosperity and resolve systemic problems.

Just as business leaders of publicly traded companies publish annual reports, the Governor should annually publish New York State's rankings among the 50 states with regard to:

1) Four Year Population Growth,
2) Four Year Personal Income Growth,
3) Percent of the Population Employed,
4) Percent of the Population without Health Insurance,
5) Percent of the Population Living in Poverty,
6) Per Pupil Education Cost,
7) High School Graduation Rates,
8) Average Math & Verbal SAT Scores,
9) Average Commute Times, and
10) The Composite Average of these Nine Benchmarks.

Similarly, just as business leaders' compensation is based on their performance, base state leaders' compensation on their performance (I-5).

For example, when New York State's composite ranking is 40th or worse, elected representatives might earn $50,000 on average, whereas upon achieving a ranking or 10th or better, they might earn $500,000 on average.

When comparison rankings are not high nor improving, voters should remove the governor and majority party incumbents. Even though we like them, and a challenger is not of our registered party, we need to fire poor performance. The well-being of millions of people must take precedence over our personal feelings towards our representatives.

Public Sector Borrowing and Spending Limits

Table 10 indicates that from 1992 to 2002, mostly years that Pataki, Bruno, and Silver held the reins of power, inflation was 28% while State Spending grew 55%, State Debt 49%, Local Government Spending 49%, and Public Education Expenditures 32%.

Growth of State Spending, State Debt, Local Government Spending, and Public Education Expenditures grew 75-100% faster than the inflation rate. The growth of State and Local Spending and Debt is clearly not sustainable. Over time, people's disposable income stagnates, and businesses and good paying jobs flee.

Table 10: Inflation and New York State's Per Capita Public Sector Growth 1992-2002

Inflation[a]	28%
State Spending[b]	55%
State Debt[b]	49%
Local Government Spending[b]	49%
Medicaid Expenditures 1993-2002[c]	107%
Public Education Expenditures[b]	32%

U.S. Department of Commerce, Bureau of Economic Analysis;
[a]U.S. Department of Labor, Bureau of Labor Statistics; [b]U.S. Bureau of the Census; [c]A Statistical View of the United States: State Rankings 1996 & 2005, Morgan Quitno.

The leaders recklessly spend state revenues and then borrow to resolve budget shortfalls. The Constitution requires that voters approve all state debt. The governor and majority party leaders skirt the constitution and use some 650 public authorities to regularly borrow without voter approval. From 1997 to 2000, they had public authorities borrow $1.2 billion to finance member items.[6] *Their shortsighted and undisciplined use of debt raises the future cost of government.*

From 1994 to 2003 the State Debt grew at a rate over 2 times the inflation rate plus the population growth rate. New York State debt service costs taxpayers $3.6 billion each year. Public debt is now 2.5 times the voter approved budget debt.[7]

The data suggests that public education contains spending far better than state and local governments. Public education is required to gain taxpayer approval on all spending. The residents of New York State would be better served by a similar mechanism to moderate state and local government borrowing and spending. New York State needs a constitutional amendment limiting the growth of per capita state and local government borrowing and spending to the inflation rate, unless a majority of the voters approve a larger increase in a public referendum (I-6).

This initiative would positively affect New York's economy more than any other. The amendment could be enacted by the New York Legislature, a Constitutional Convention, or residents via Voter Initiative, if New York State had Voter Initiative. By focusing on per-capita borrowing and spending, the growth limitation includes adjustments for increases and decreases in population.

Reining in Medicaid

Medicaid was created in 1965 by the federal government to provide medical services for poor people. The program is managed by the states. Some services are required by the federal government and some are added by the state. The beneficiaries do not receive the money. The hospitals, physicians, nursing homes, pharmacies, and other medical providers receive the $46 billion New York spends on Medicaid each year.

Nineteen percent of New York State's population now receives Medicaid compared to eleven percent of Minnesota population. In addition, New York per recipient benefits are nearly twice the national average. Twice as many people receive twice as much per recipient![8] From 1993-2002, per-capita Medicaid costs increased 107%, while inflation increased 24%.[9] Medicaid expenditures increase four times the inflation rate!

Unlike other states, New York has no years of residency eligibility requirement. The state allows people with incomes and assets above the poverty level to qualify for Medicaid. The state allows a married adult to be covered regardless of the spouse's income and assets. People may transfer their assets to family members at any time and receive coverage for homecare services. The state specifies no preferred drug list.[10]

We want to take care of the poor, but we do not want people with means to live-off the system. For in doing so, we lessen our capacity to care for the poor.

Fixing Medicaid is largely a manner of learning from other states and taking away the blank check that our elected officials think they possess. We need to require three years of state residency, and poverty level incomes and assets, for people to be eligible for Medicaid. We need to include spouses' income and assets, and a 5 year look-back on an applicant's assets in the eligibility determination for homecare and skilled nursing facilities (I-7).

Consolidate Local Government

New York's system of local government is redundant and expensive. *New York has 689 school districts, but 1609 county, city, town, and village governments.*[11] *This is at least 920 too many local governments.*

I reside in Baldwinsville, a relatively small community of 20,000 people. It is typical of many New York communities. It has one school district, but three local governments, when one would suffice. Similarly, every major upstate city is surrounded by a county, duplicating most of the city government's functions.

The high cost and inefficiency of our local governments become apparent by benchmarking them against local governments in other states. In contrast to Minnesota, a state that is doing remarkably well by all measures, New York has 20% more local government employees per 10,000 people and pays them on average some 30% more. Local government costs New Yorkers 50% more than it costs residents of Minnesota and most other states (Table 11).

Table 11: Local Government Employees

	Minnesota	NYS
Number of Employees Per 10,000 People	412	492
Average Annual Earnings	$42,747	$54,698
Per-Capita Cost	$1,761	$2,691

Statistical View of the United States: State Rankings 2005, Morgan Quitno.

The province of Ontario very successfully consolidated its local governments in the 1970s. Toronto's transformation into a world class city started with the consolidation of its local governments.

Local politics are such that the local municipalities do not consolidate on their own. New York State should force the 1609 county, city, town, and village governments to consolidate into 689 local governments that are analogous to the 689 school districts (I-8).

Interstate Benchmarks and Performance Based Compensation, Public Sector Borrowing and Spending Limits, Reining in Medicaid, and Consolidation of Local Government comprise my Taxpayer Bill of Rights. The first initiative alters the focus of elected officials from vested interests to citizen interests. The latter three initiatives reduce public sector burdens on the private sector, enabling New York businesses to compete with businesses of other states and countries.

These initiatives not only improve New York's business climate, but they generate resources to improve inner-city and rural schools and the decaying transportation infrastructure. As businesses become more competitive, they and their employees pay more taxes. As New York's Medicaid costs become more similar to those of other states, resources are freed to address education and transportation needs. The Taxpayer Bill of Rights initiatives are essential to addressing New York's systemic income, employment, healthcare, poverty, education, and transportation challenges.

Part IV: Inner-City & Rural Student Bill of Rights

Whoso [does not learn] in his youth, loses the past and is dead for the future.
— *Euripides*

Equitably Fund All Public Schools

No other system has more impact on the futures of individuals, families, the state, and the country than our educational system. Education affects our civility, health, careers, living standards, children, and the state's and country's competitiveness. Of all the systems in our lives, education should be our best performing system.

In New York State, we spend 50% per pupil more than the national average to educate our children, yet we rank 44th among the fifty states in the percent of students graduating from high school and 43rd in average SAT scores. In this information and global economy age to have 41% of our students not graduating from high school is tragic.

Many of New York State's schools, administrators, and teachers are outstanding. The deficiencies reside largely with a portion of the districts, administrators, and teachers. Yet, the deficiencies are numerous and substantial enough to significantly lower the state's rankings.

Ask an elected official about the sorry state of New York education and the response is that "we have a diverse population." Is this code for "we have large minority populations and do not expect them to do well," or that "it's somebody else's problem and I am not going to spend my political capital to address it"?

The number one problem with New York's public education system is the state funds elementary and secondary education with too little state revenue and too much local tax revenue. This practice creates tremendous disparity in the quality of our school districts. It causes inner-city and rural schools to have inferior facilities, textbooks, and curriculum. Inner-city and rural schools constantly lose the best administrators and teachers to wealthier suburban school districts. It causes poorer school districts to graduate fewer of its students and to have significantly lower SAT scores. It makes property taxes unaffordable for many seniors and low income residents. It causes businesses to bear property taxes, which makes them uncompetitive with businesses in other states.

The State Education Department indicates that the difference in per pupil spending between the 10th percentile and the 90th percentile districts is almost 85%![12] In 2004, the lowest decile spent an estimated $8,000 and the highest decile $15,000 per student.

To adequately and equitably fund school districts, as well as keep property taxes affordable for seniors and businesses, the state should establish a minimum per pupil funding standard. It should cap the education portion of property taxes that *senior citizens, farmers, and businesses* pay to 2% of their property values. It should expect local property taxes to cover an amount equivalent to 2% of a district's property values. The state should then fund every school district so that its total local, federal, and state funding meets the minimum per pupil funding standard (I-9). A school district could increase its local funding above 2% of their property values provided residents approved the proposed district budget. Districts' property values, not local revenues, would affect its state funding.

The state can find the money to better fund inner-city and rural schools from the Medicaid black hole. From 1993-2003, New York State's population increased 5% and Medicaid enrollment 33%. From 1993-2002, inflation was 24% and Medicaid expenditures increased 107%. In 2002, Social Security and Medicaid spending for New York residents, which didn't even exist prior to 1930, was $68 billion, while spending on primary and secondary education was $38 billion.[13]

As a culture, we are deploying too many of our resources for the elderly and dependent, relative to the education of our youth. We are not doing this consciously; rather, self-serving majority party leaders respond to the campaign contributions of the healthcare unions and ignore the powerless inner-city and rural youth. Inner-city and rural youth have no advocates, do not vote, and do not make campaign contributions.

In my mind, the failure of our elected officials to control the growth of Medicaid enrollment and expenditures, as well as to deploy more resources to inner-city and rural schools, is short-sighted, derelict, and unconscionable.

Raising money for education primarily from local property taxes rather than state income taxes, results in geographic disadvantage causing educational disadvantage. One generation's unfortunate circumstances become transferred to the next generation, not only at home, but also at the public schools.

Strengthen School Administrations

The second problem of New York's education system is that school administrations are weak. *The state teachers' union that is superbly funded, organized, and active, eliminates tools that administrators need to create excellent schools.*

School administrators, as leaders of any organization, need to readily remove poor performers and reward the better performers. The tenure system and administrator and teacher unions inhibit this. School boards and superintendents must devote countless hours over 3-5 years to remove a marginally performing administrator or teacher. Because administrator and teacher salaries for the five years prior to retirement determine lifelong pensions, unions place immense pressure on school districts to reward seniority rather than merit.

Jack Welch, CEO at General Electric, took a mediocre performing colossus and transformed it into a phenomenon. Key to General Electric's ascendancy was his insistence on identifying and rewarding people's performance. Each year he required his leaders to place those reporting to them into one of three groups, the top performing 20%, the middle performing 70%, and the poorest performing 10%. He gave the top 20% raises 2-3 times the middle group's raises. He gave no raise to the poorest performing 10%, encouraging them to find work elsewhere.[14]

The combination of tenure, protective union work rules, and seniority-based raises for administrators and teachers in New York State public schools offers administrators and teachers incentives to work hard initially and occasionally shields them from an unreasonable school board member or parent. However they also eliminate incentives for them to perform at high levels upon receiving tenure and make it impractical for school leaders to remove poor performing personnel.

Consider for a moment that every time tenure, union work rules, and seniority-based raises keep a poor performing teacher employed for 20-40 years, some 2000-4000 students' lives are negatively impacted. When a poor performing administrator remains employed, who in turn protects 50 poor performing teachers, even more students' lives are negatively impacted. This is not supposition, New York's social services roles and prisons are filled with hundreds of thousands of individuals that our education system has failed.

Mr. Welch's approach, applied to our public schools, would dramatically improve the lives of tens of thousands of youth and eventually their children. The tenure system and the largely seniority-based raise system for administrators and teachers needs to be swept into the ash bin of history. School districts need to devote more resources for hiring and rewarding excellent administrators and teachers and they need to be able to more easily remove poor performing personnel (I-10a).

When a dysfunctional school board exists, which hires dysfunctional administrators, who in turn hire mediocre teachers, thousands of students' are irrevocably harmed. To address poor performing districts, New York State has in place a Registration Review Process. Any school may be subject to the review process if 90% of students fail to score above state benchmarks; there are persistent parent complaints; or conditions threaten the health, safety, or educational welfare of students.

Identified schools are reviewed by an outside team of board of education members, superintendents, teachers, education experts, and parents. Once the review team findings are submitted to the state, the district's superintendent develops a corrective action plan. A state education department staff member is assigned to the district to ensure the school implements the plan. This is an excellent program that needs strengthen and additional resources (I-10b).

The Inner-city and Rural Student Bill of Rights, comprised of the Equitably Fund All Public Schools and Strengthen School Administrations initiatives, is fundamental to the future of New York State. These initiatives would improve the lives of hundreds of thousands of youth and their future children. They would reduce drug and alcohol dependencies, teenage births, and crime rates. They would increase the employed proportion of our population and reduce future social service roles and expenditures. The initiatives would improve our state's and country's ability to compete in the marketplace. They would increase every New Yorker's standard of living and quality of life.

Part V: Business Bill of Rights

With China and India supplying low cost, high quality intellect, goods, and services, we must adapt just to maintain the status quo. Only countries, states, and companies that collaborate, innovate, and lower costs will prosper.
— Thoughts from *The World is Flat*, Thomas L. Friedman

As water flows downhill, so talent, capital, and jobs flow to favorable business climates in a global economy. A region's well-being depends not only on its corporate strengths, but on government's ability to create favorable business conditions. These favorable business conditions include: minimal and reasonable regulations; untaxed business inputs; low cost water, sanitary, electrical, and gas services; an efficient transportation infrastructure; and minimally taxed profits. Embracing this fact significantly increases the likelihood of a thriving economy and an improving quality of life. Ignoring this fact guarantees declining relative standards of living and the eventual exodus of children from the region.

New York's loss of hundreds of thousands of construction and manufacturing jobs contributes greatly to the state's low employment, high poverty, and large Medicaid population. Since the 1960s, New York lost over 1 million manufacturing jobs alone, which were many of its best paying blue collar jobs.[14] The loss was much more significant than it seems, as some 2.5 other jobs accompany each manufacturing job.[15] This 3.5 million manufacturing related job loss was devastating, given only 9.4 million people are employed in the state.[16] The state's loss of jobs has left hundreds of thousands of people in New York marooned and permanently unemployed.

Competitive Electrical Costs

Given a state blessed with more than its fair share of low cost hydro and nuclear power, why do businesses and consumers on average pay 57% more for electricity than they would in other states? Ask someone in government or the industry to explain this and they will give you numerous reasons. Each responsible person will blame someone else and suggest nothing can be done about the higher costs.

Although New York taxes electricity, the taxes no longer are the primary cause of the state's high electrical prices. New York electrical prices are high for the following two reasons: (1) the Governor, the Senate and Assembly Leadership, and the Public Service Commission do a horrible job of regulating the utilities, and (2) they obstruct the utilities' ability to build capacity and address transmission bottlenecks.

In 2001, New Yorkers spent $16.4 billion on electricity.[18] In New York State, electricity for industrial, commercial, and residential use runs 57% over the national average.[19] *If businesses and consumers bought the same amount of electricity at average national prices, they would save $6.0 billion annually!*

If our business, Plainville Farms, bought electricity priced at the national average, it would save over $200,000 each year. The savings would cause us to add $20,000 to our employees' bonuses and pay $70,000 more in federal taxes and $14,000 more in state taxes. New York receives back form the federal government 80% of the federal taxes collected in the state. Thus, $56,000 of the $70,000 in federal taxes would come back to the state. We would invest $96,000 more in the business. The additional money invested would enable us to borrow and invest a second $96,000 in the business.

In summary, the $200,000 savings causes the company to employ additional people, improve existing employees' compensation, and provide directly and indirectly $282,000 ($20,000 + $56,000 + $14,000 + $96,000 + $96,000) of economic stimulus to the state.

Competitively priced electricity and these series of events multiplied thousand of times in other businesses across the state would strengthen businesses, create jobs, raise wages, and raise government revenues. They would provide a $6 billion annual economic stimulus to the state economy that would compound overtime.

New York could realize all of these benefits if its leaders did just an average rather than poor job of regulating the state's electrical utility monopolies. Shamefully, our state leadership prefers economic programs that generate campaign contributions over properly managing the utility monopolies.

The Governor and Senate and Assembly Energy Committees should appoint an independent commission to research and recommend legislation to expand the state's electrical generation and transmission capacity. Our governor and legislature should initiate the construction of additional generation capacity and the modernization of the state's electrical grid. They should predicate a utility's authorization to service an area on its delivery of electricity at costs below the national average (I-11a).

Workers' Compensation Reform

In some sense, New York has encouraged the departure of one million of its best blue collar jobs with its Workers' Compensation Program. No other reason for leaving the state is so frequently cited by manufacturers.

Rates for Workers' Compensation have come down since 1995, but the assessment imposed by New York has continuously increased. The average settlement of a Workers' Compensation case in New York is still 72% above the national average, $11,793 versus $6,552. As shocking, the maximum weekly benefit paid to injured workers is the 45th lowest in the nation.[20] Currently, 14% of the cases where benefits are not defined account for 77% of the total system costs.[21] *Only New York could devise a Workers' Compensation Program that costs employers more and pays injured employees less.*

Unlike Workers' Compensation in other states, the problems with Workers' Compensation in New York are: (1) objective guidelines to assess medical impairment are not spelled out in the statute, (2) awards for many injuries are not defined in the statute, (3) permanent partial disability awards are made for life, and (4) no offset is made to Workers' Compensation benefits when recipients receive social security and pension benefits.[22]

System costs could be dramatically lowered for employers, and weekly benefits increased for injured employees, by enacting objective Workers' Compensation guidelines to assess medical impairment; defining awards for injuries in the statue; and only providing compensation until an injured party is eligible for Social Security (I-11b).

A Competitive Tort Environment

Litigation costs ultimately are not paid by wealthy individuals, large corporations, insurance companies, and municipalities; they are paid by consumers and taxpayers. The awards that seemingly deep pockets pay pass to consumers and taxpayers in the form of higher insurance costs, product or service prices, and government tax rates.

New York produces fewer products and services, because of its higher litigation costs. The production of fewer products and services limits job opportunities and income growth.

The New York State Builders Association indicates that CGU, CAN, Great American, Kemper, Royal, St. Paul-Travelers, and Zurich insurance companies no longer offer general liability insurance to contractors in New York. Contractors are left with only three insurers.[23]

A New York State court's liberal interpretation of an antiquated liability law changed the liability insurance dynamic in 1999. The Builder's Association indicates that general liability insurance costs have increased from $2.76 per $1000 for coverage in 1999 to $14.45 per $1000 in 2004. 2004 general liability premium quotes for the same class of builders in the Northeast are: New York $64,000, Pennsylvania $13,300, New Jersey $9,900, and Connecticut $6,400. The five year increase adds an estimated $10,000 to the cost of a new home.[24]

To rein in excessive litigation costs, The Business Council of New York indicates the New York legislature should enact several of the following common sense Tort Reforms: a) Require the court system to report suit type, number, and average award amounts, so elected officials and the public can assess litigation policies. b) End the NYS only practice of injured construction workers receiving both workers' compensation and litigation awards. c) Eliminate awards to plaintiffs who cause their own injury by failing to follow well established safety policies, drunkenness, or drug use. d) Limit the number of years that manufacturers and contractors are liable for products and work and do not juxtapose today's standards on yesterday's products and work. e) End the practice where juries force marginally involved parties with deep pockets to pay awards, and cap pain and suffering awards at $1 million per plaintiff. f) Enact a sliding fee schedule for litigation, where the plaintiffs' attorneys receive

30% of the first $250,000 of an award, 20% of amounts over $500,000, and 10% of amounts over $1 million (I-12). [25]

These initiatives further accountability and justice. They reduce legal mischief and some of the windfall that trial lawyers realize. They lower health costs and enable employers to provide health insurance to more people. These initiatives better align New York liability costs with those of other states, furthering the growth of jobs and people's incomes.

Competitive Energy and Workers' Compensation Costs and a Competitive Tort Environment are the initiatives of The Business Bill of Rights. Implementation of these initiatives along with lower property taxes would significantly strengthen New York businesses, enabling many more to remain and grow within the state. The additional business activity and good paying jobs increase people's incomes and government tax revenues. If the Assembly Democrats and Senate Republicans truly serve New York State's working people, they will address the states high electrical, workers' compensation, and liability costs in a real and meaningful way.

Part VI: Igniting an Economic Renaissance

When you have duly arrayed your "facts" in logical order, lo, it is like an oil-lamp that you have made, filled and trimmed, but which sheds no light unless first you light it.

— *Saint Exupery*

Your Involvement is Essential

Laws in New York State are for sale to the highest bidder. Our state's leadership ignores endless conflicts of interest and operates much like the leadership of a banana republic. To take the number one economy in the world in 1950 to its present 44th place among the 50 states verges on the criminal. Below appear the Bills of Rights and Initiatives that will make representatives more effective agents of the citizenry and will transform New York from a state in decline to a state in ascendancy.

Voter Bill of Rights
Voter Initiative
Non-partisan Voting Districts
Citizen Based Campaign Financing
Senate & Assembly Rule Reforms

Taxpayer Bill of Rights
Interstate Benchmarks & Performance Based Compensation
Public Sector Borrowing and Spending Limits
Reining in Medicaid
Consolidation of Local Government

Inner-city & Rural Student Bill of Rights
Equitably Fund All Public Schools
Strengthen School Administrations

Business Bill of Rights
Competitive Electrical and Workers' Compensation Costs
A Competitive Tort Environment

The four Bill of Rights and twelve Initiatives provide in excess of a $30 billion dollar annual economic stimulus to the New York economy that compounds over time. They improve job opportunities, increase personal incomes, improve education for numerous children, lift people out of poverty, and enable businesses to provide health insurance to far more employees. In just a few years, they would dramatically improve New York State's rankings in all of the listed categories.

Special interests will fight these common sense initiatives with millions of dollars of campaign contributions, fear mongering, and smear campaigns. They will fight them, because they upset their cozy and lucrative arrangements with our state leaders. Only yours and hundreds of thousands of other voters' involvement will overcome the special interests.

Please share "Creating Prosperous New York State" with your friends. Phone, email, or write the Governor, Senate Majority Leader, Assembly Speaker, and your Senate and Assembly Representatives. Ask them to support these twelve initiatives. A form letter appears on the following page. Addresses and a form letter may be found at FreeNYS.org.

Vote for Senate Democrats and Republican Assembly Representatives. Only support majority party representatives if they actively support these initiatives through voice and deed. Beware of deceptive lip service to reform.

With your help we will focus state leaders on improving the lives of all New York citizens. We will unravel the Gordian knot. We will eliminate conflicts of interest, create jobs, and grow personal incomes. We will provide health insurance for more people, improve inner-city and rural education, and upgrade our transportation system. We will create a future for our children and grandchildren that will include New York State.

To: _____

_____

_____

From: _____

_____

_____

Date: _____

Re: *Creating a Prosperous New York State*

    I would like to encourage you to read Mark Bitz's *Creating a Prosperous New York State* and implement the twelve initiatives.

    Please benchmark New York State's performance against other states, listen to normal every day citizens, and work with your colleagues for the common good.

    Provide all New York State children with an excellent education.

    Do not mortgage our children's futures nor drive capital, wealth, talent and youth from the state with excessive taxes.

    Finally, create a state where businesses thrive, good paying jobs are abundant, and our children want to reside.

_____
Signature

Initiative Summary

Voter Bill of Rights

I-1 Voter Initiative

Enact a process where citizens who obtain 500 supporting signatures in each of New York's 62 counties can propose laws to the voters in general elections.

I-2 Non-partisan Voting Districts

Set up an independent commission of retired judges to oversee the development of a computer algorithm to draw Senate and Assembly districts, maximizing the use of county and township lines and minimizing the number of lines to draw each district.

I-3 Citizen Based Campaign Financing

Allow candidates to raise campaign funds only during the ten months prior to an election; require them to return any unused campaign funds to donors after an election; bar businesses, unions, PACs, and all organizations from making campaign contributions; and limit individual contributions to $100 per candidate per year.

I-4 Senate & Assembly Rule Reforms

a) Treat all senators and assembly members equally within their respective houses with regard to their budget, staff, member item money, and compensation.

b) Require any exceptions made for house and committee leaders to be approved by two-thirds of the members in both the Senate and Assembly.

c) Empower committee chairs to employ and terminate staff; require committees to hold a public hearing upon the request of one quarter of the committee members; and require committee chairs to hold votes to release each bill referred to the committee 60 days prior to the end of a session.

d) Make the votes part of the public record.

e) Require a complete committee report for all bills favorably reported by a committee; require a house floor vote on every bill that is favorably discharged from a committee within 60 days; and convene conference committees upon the request of either of a bill's major sponsors.

Taxpayer Bill of Rights

I- 5   Interstate Benchmarks & Performance Based Compensation

Require the governor to annually publish New York State's Ranking among the 50 states with regard to:

1) Four Year Population Growth,
2) Four Year Personal Income Growth,
3) Percent of the Population Employed,
4) Percent of the Population w/o Health Insurance,
5) Percent of the Population Living in Poverty,
6) Per Pupil Education Cost,
7) High School Graduation Rates,
8) Average Math & Verbal SAT Scores,
9) Average Commute Times, and
10) The Composite Average of these Nine Benchmarks.

Base state leaders' compensation on their performance.

I-6 Public Sector Borrowing and Spending Limits

Limit the per-capita state and local government borrowing and spending to the inflation rate unless a majority of the voters approve a larger increase in a public referendum.

I-7 Reining in Medicaid

Require three years of state residency, and poverty level incomes and assets, for people to be eligible for Medicaid. Include spouses' income and assets, and a 5 year look-back on an applicant's assets in the eligibility determination.

I-8 Consolidation of Local Government

Require the 1609 county, city, town, and village governments to consolidate to some 689 local governments that are analogous to the 689 school districts.

Inner-City & Rural Student Bill of Rights

I-9 Equitably Fund All Public Schools

Establish a minimum per pupil funding standard. Cap the education portion of property taxes that senior citizens, farmers, and businesses pay to 2% of their property values. Expect local property taxes to cover an amount equivalent to 2% of a district's property values. Fund every school district so that its total local, federal, and state funding meets the minimum per pupil funding standard.

I-10 Strengthen School Administrations

a) End the tenure system for public school administrators and teachers and implement a primarily performance based raise system for them. Enable school districts to more easily remove poor performing personnel.

b) Strengthen and expand the New York State School District Registration Review Process.

Business Bill of Rights

I-11 Competitive Electrical and Workers' Compensation Costs

a) Authorize the construction of additional generation capacity and the modernization of the state's electrical grid. Predicate a utilities authorization to service an area on its ability to deliver electricity at costs below the national average.

b) Enact objective Workers' Compensation guidelines to assess medical impairment. Define awards for injuries in the statue. Only provide compensation until an injured party is eligible for Social Security.

I-12 A Competitive Tort Environment

a) Require the court system to report suit type, number, and average award amounts, so elected officials and the public can assess litigation policies.

b) End the NYS only practice of injured construction workers receiving both workers' compensation and litigation awards.

c) Eliminate awards to plaintiffs who cause their own injury by failing to follow well established safety policies, drunkenness, or drug use.

d) Limit the number of years that manufacturers and contractors are liable for products and work, and do not juxtapose today's standards on yesterday's products and work.

e) End the practice where juries force marginally involved parties with deep pockets to pay awards, and cap pain and suffering awards at $1 million per plaintiff.

f) Enact a sliding fee schedule for litigation, where the plaintiffs' attorneys receive 30% of the first $250,000 of an award, 20% of amounts over $500,000, and 10% of amounts over $1 million.

Table References & Notes

Table 1   U.S. Department of Commerce Bureau of Economic Analysis, www.bea.doc.gov/bea/regional/bearfacts/statebf.cfm;
A Statistical View of the United States: State Rankings 2005, Morgan Quitno, pp. 97, 128, 132, 133, 140, 169, 366, 427, 495, 544, 559.

Table 2   New York Commission on Lobbying, www.nylobby.state.ny.us/annreport/03artext.html.

Table 3   *Just the Facts*, The Business Council of New York State, www.ppinys.org/reports/jtf.htm;
A Statistical View of the United States: State Rankings 2005, Morgan Quitno, p. 295.

Table 4   "Restructuring in the Manufacturing Workforce: New York State and the Nation," Buffalo Branch, Federal Reserve of New York State, *Regional Economy, Winter 2004*; U.S. Department of Commerce, Bureau of Economic Analysis, www.bea.gov/regional/spi/drill.cfm;
A Statistical View of the United States: State Rankings 1995, Morgan Quitno, p. 495; *A Statistical View of the United States: State Rankings 2005*, Morgan Quitno, pp. 463, 473, 514; U.S. Bureau of the Census, www.census.gov/popest/archives/1990s/stas/st-99-16.txt.

Table 5   "Reform New York: Ten Steps for Change," New York Public Interest Research Group, Albany, NY, p.3.

Table 6   U.S. Department of Commerce Bureau of Economic Analysis, www.bea.doc.gov/bea/regional/bearfacts/statebf.cfm, www.bea.doc/cea/dn/nipaweb/TableView.asp#Mid;
U.S. Bureau of the Census, www.census.gov/statab/hist/HS-35.pdf.

Table 7   U.S. Department of Commerce Bureau of Economic Analysis, www.bea.doc.gov/bea/regional/bearfacts/statebf.cfm;
U.S. Department of Labor Bureau of Labor Statistics, www.bls.gov/cpi/home.htm#overview;
Downstate is defined as Putnam, Westchester, Rockland, Nassau, Suffolk, Bronx, New York, Richmond, Kings, and Queens Counties.

Table 8   "PAC-ing IT IN: Political Action Committees Contributions in New York State 2004," New York Public Interest Research Group, Albany, NY.

Table 9   U.S. Department of Commerce Bureau of Economic Analysis, www.bea.doc.gov/bea/regional/bearfacts/statebf.cfm;
A Statistical View of the United States: State Rankings 2005, Morgan Quitno, pp. 128, 132, 133, 140, 169, 366, 495, 544, and 559.

Table 10 U.S. Department of Commerce, Bureau of Economic Analysis, www.bea.gov/regional/spi/drill.cfm; U.S. Department of Labor Bureau of Labor Statistics, www.bls.gov/cpi/cgi-bin/cpicalc.pl;

U.S. Bureau of the Census, www.census.gov/govs/www/state/html; www.census.gov/govs/www/estimate92.html; www.census.gov/govs/www/school.html; *A Statistical View of the United States: State Rankings 1996*, Morgan Quitno, p. 501; *A Statistical View of the United States: State Rankings 2005*, Morgan Quitno, p. 512.

Table 11 *A Statistical View of the United States: State Rankings 2005*, Morgan Quitno, pp. 359, 360, and 427.

Endnotes

[1] *"Reform New York: 10 Steps on the Path to Change Albany,"* Blair Horner, New York Public Interest Research Group, October, 2004, pp. 2-7; "Issue: Redistricting Reform," New York Public Interest Research Group, April, 2005.

[2] "Packing a Punch," Terry M. Moe, *Wall Street Journal*, August 25, 2005, p. A8.

[3] "The New York State Legislative Process: An Evaluation and Blueprint for Reform, Executive Summary," Jeremy Creelan, New York University Brennan Center for Justice, 2004, pp. 2-3.

[4] "The New York State Legislative Process: An Evaluation and Blueprint for Reform, Executive Summary," Jeremy Creelan, New York University Brennan Center for Justice, 2004, pp.2-8.

[5] *A Statistical View of the United States: State Rankings 2005,* Morgan Quitno, pp. 132, 133, and 140.

[6] "New York's Slush Funds: Albany's Secret Funds Put Taxpayers in the Dark and in Debt," *The Post-Standard*, Syracuse, NY, October 17, 2004.

[7] "New York State's Debt Policy: A Need for Reform, February 2005," New York Office of the State Comptroller.

[8] *A Statistical View of the United States: State Rankings 2005,* Morgan Quitno, pp. 427, 514 and 515.

[9] Department of Labor Bureau of Labor Statistics, www.bls.gov/cpi/cgi-bin/cpicalc.pl; *A Statistical View of the United States: State Rankings 1996*, Morgan Quitno, p. 501; *A Statistical View of the United States: State Rankings 2005*, Morgan Quitno, p. 512.

[10]"Medicaid Inc: Why New York has the Nation's Most Expensive Medicaid Program," The Rochester Business Alliance and Rump Group.

[11]Glen Falls Post Star, Editorial, 6/30/05.

[12]"*State Aid to Schools: A Primer,*" The University of the State of New York, State Education Department, Fiscal Analysis and Research Unit, November, 2002; Standard & Poors School Evaluation Services, www.schoolmatters.com.

[13]*A Statistical View of the United States: State Rankings 2005,* Morgan Quitno, pp. 140, 503, and 512.

[14]Welch, Jack, *Jack: Straight from the Gut,* Warner Books, Inc, New York, NY, Chapter 11.

[15]"Restructuring in the Manufacturing Workforce: New York State and the Nation," *Regional Economy, Winter 2004,* Buffalo Branch, Federal Reserve of New York State.

[16] "The Facts about Modern Manufacturing," National Association of Manufacturing.

[17]*A Statistical View of the United States: State Rankings 2005,* Morgan Quitno, p.169.

[18]*A Statistical View of the United States: State Rankings 2005,* Morgan Quitno, p. 205.

[19]*Just the Facts*, The Business Council of New York State, www.ppinys.org/reports/jtf.htm.

[20] AFL-CIO, www.aflcio.org/issues/safety/wc/upload/comptable.pdf.

[21] "*News July 2005*," The Business Council of New York State, Inc.

[22] Manufacuters Association of Central New York 2005-2006 Public Policy Agenda, p. 4.

[23] New York State Builders Association, Inc., Memorandum, "General Liability Insurance Crisis-Economic Impact," March, 2003.

[24] New York State Builders Association, Inc., "Memorandum in Support Senate Bill, S.3823 (Volker) and Assembly Bill, A.2946-A (Morelle)," May, 2005.

[25] "*An Accident and a Dream*," The Business Council of New York State, Inc.

More Praise for Creating a Prosperous New York State

    I have included several comments from a diverse group of leaders of large constituencies regarding the appeal of this book's content to demonstrate people's pervasive disgust with our state's leaders and their desire for improvement.

Every concerned citizen of this once great New York State should carry this book in their hip pocket. Rarely have the chronic ills of our current state been so succinctly enumerated, making it readily apparent that the remedial steps suggested are sure to succeed . . . but only if we have the will to see them through to fruition.

    — *Roger Bogsted, Nassau County, Conservative Party Chair*

Mark is a sober, sensible businessman, who understands that New York's competitiveness problems are best understood by highlighting our anemic performance in job and wealth creation compared to other states with comparable circumstances and challenges. Everyone interested in understanding the extent to which New York's problems are self-inflicted will benefit from this book.

    — *Matthew Maguire, Moderator, Upstateblog.net*

Mark understands the complex workings of NYS government and offers excellent insights into the economic and political challenges facing our state. He proposes intelligent, politically feasible, common sense solutions. The book is an essential roadmap to a strong and prosperous New York. It is indispensable reading for all New Yorkers, especially elected officials.

    — *Michael Benjamin, Chairman, Save New York, Inc.*

Mark is a leading voice in the movement to create a more responsive and responsible government, and more prosperous future. This book outlines some of our greatest challenges, the reasons for those challenges, and possible solutions.

    — *Dave Valesky, NYS Senator*

Mark hits the nail on the head in his assessment of NYS's once strong economy and the need for reform in Albany. I applaud him for his insightful commentary.

—*Jeff Brown, Assemblyman*

This is a must read for everyone who loves New York. Well researched and organized, Mark has created a blueprint to return our state to the economic prominence it once enjoyed.

—*Harold King, Executive VP, The Council of Industry of S.E. New York*

Everyday manufacturers see the devastating impact of increasing costs to their businesses. One cannot read this book without agreeing with Mark - New York State needs reform now if it wants to maintain and grow high paying jobs in its vital manufacturing sector.

—*Randy Wolken, Executive Director, Manufacturers Association of CNY*

I commend you for having the dedication as a private citizen and business owner to address the issues plaguing New York State. Your synopsis of the situation provides an opportunity to address the impediments that prevent our economic prominence.

—*Irwin Davis, President, The Syracuse Metropolitan Development Agency*

Mark offers an objective analysis of the difficulties New York businesses face and the implications to all state residents. There is no spin, no exaggeration, just the facts from a person who cares about his business, employees, community, and state.

—*Greg Harden, President of Harden Furniture*

This book should become a New York Times best seller. We need more New Yorkers to take its message to heart before the tax base erodes to the point that New York becomes little more than one giant welfare state.

—*Milt Stevenson Jr., Principle of Anoplate*

The book's comparison of New York and Minnesota provide proof that it is not the snow that drives business away from the state; rather it is the snow job the citizens receive from Pataki, Bruno, and Silver.

—*Thomas Waring, The Waring Financial Group*

Acknowledgements

I would like to thank my beautiful wife, Leokadia, and wonderful sons, Karl and Asher, for putting up with my mental and physical absences as I research, write, and speak about Creating a Prosperous New York State. I also thank the extraordinary Plainville Farms and Central New York Feeds management teams and team members who carry on so well in my absence.

Special thanks to the following people for their support and help in preparing and distributing this document: Bill Burrows, Joe Coleman, Roxanne Parmele, Kemper Matt, Steve McMahon of Inside Out, Norm Poltenson, Barb Quijano, Patty Schuster, Bella Stahl, Don Sundman, Sherri Woods, and Friends at Dupli – Kemper Matt Jr., Jeff Degre, Nick Ugliuzza, Jim Gosson and Caroline Gosson.

I also wish to thank the following people for all of their encouragement: Mark Alesee; Bill Allyn; Esther, Alycia and Martin Anthony; Will Barclay; Barbara Bartoletti; Anthony Baynes; Dave Barclay; Michael Benjamin; Robert Bogsted; Jeff Brown; Mary Ellen Burris; Jeremy Creelan; Jeanne Dangle; Irwin Davis; David Duerr; John Doyle; Jack Endryck; John Faso; Dan Fisher; Jay Gallagher; Tom Golisano; Bruce Grieshaber; Greg Harden; Kristen Heath; Patrick Hooker; Harold King; David Klein; John Lincoln; David Little; Michael Long; Pat Manning; Pat Mannion; Matt Maguire; E.J. McMahon; Charlie Nesbitt; David Paterson; Nick Pirro; David Spence; Jim Sollecito; Milt Stevenson Jr.; Tom Suozzi; Dave Valesky; Jim Walsh; Bob Ward; Tom Waring; Bill Weld; Randy Wolken and Andy Zaplatynsky.

Here's to some of the true warriors who fight every day to make New York State more prosperous and more democratic: Mark Alesse, Barbara Bartoletti, Michael Benjamin, Jeff Brown, Jeremy Creelan, Tom Golisano, Blair Horner, Rachel Leon, Michael Long, Pat Manning, Matt McGuire, Charlie Nesbitt, Nick Pirro, Mark Schroeder, Elliot Spitzer, Tom Souzzi, and Dave Valesky.

Finally, I would like to thank some of the newspaper, radio, television, and internet professionals who have helped spread the reform message. These people include: Liz Benjamin, Lise Bang-Jenson, Tom Bauerle, Karl Bitz, Adam Chodale, Bill Colley, Mike Connor, Erin Covey, Dan Cummings, Bob Damon, Fred Dicker, Fritz Diddle, John Dye, Jay Gallagher, Mark Hamberg, Kevin Hyghland, Rick Jensen, Keith Kemp, Erik Kriss, Steve Kimatian, Bill Lemon, Nick Matchuk, Norm Poltenson, Peter Pollack, Jim Reith, Paul Riede, Steve Rogers, Curt Smith, Lisa Spitz, Joel Stashenko, Sarah Stone, Garry Togni, and Kathy Wagner.

About the Author

I own and operate a 6th generation business with about $25 million in annual sales. Our products are cutting edge and demand for them is excellent. The Workers' Compensation costs, energy costs, and taxes are some $600,000 a year more for our business in New York than they would be in other states. Every ten years our competition gains a $6 million advantage on our business. This advantage compounds over time.

When we invest $250,000 to $5 million in a structure, the next day the structure becomes worth 20% to 50% of what it cost. In other states the asset would hold or even appreciate in value. To keep the business viable, I need to invest $15 million into it over the next 10 years. If the business continues to do well, this capital will earn half the return it would earn in other states.

The 800,000 square feet of turkey barns and 75,000 square feet of processing plants are not movable or easily replaced in another state. New York's higher costs make the business unattractive to other companies in our industry. Transferring the business to my children would seem to set them up for a long swim upstream and perhaps inevitable failure.

Do we abandon our 200 wonderful team members and the $20 million our family and bank have already invested into our business and start over in another state, or do we remain in New York? Thousands of other business owners in the state face this dilemma. This is not a good situation for all New Yorkers. These words and the accompanying data should make this painfully clear. Rather than buy help from the state with large campaign contributions, or let 6 generations of incredibly hard work go down the drain, I decided to try to help New York State find its way out of this darkness and decay.